Table of Contents

What's a Wolverine?

What's the first thing you think of when you hear the word "wolverine"? Probably the X–Men movies.

But the character Wolverine started out in comic books. He first appeared in an issue of *The Incredible Hulk* in 1974.

Wolverine, the comic book character

In some X-Men movies, Wolverine is played by an Australian actor named Hugh Jackman.

What did the writer who created Wolverine have in mind? A real wolverine—a smart, strong animal with killer claws.

Since "wolverine" sounds like "wolf," you might guess that the two animals are related. But they aren't. A wolverine has much more in common with a short-tailed weasel.

A wolverine looks like a small bear with a bushy tail. It's no more than three feet long and weighs about 20 to 40 pounds.

wolverine

short-tailed weasel

All in the Family

Members of the weasel family are small with short legs. They have round ears and thick fur. They live alone most of the time and are active all year long.

sable mitt ferret

American mink

marten

7

Early Wolverines

The earliest members of the weasel family lived on Earth about 35 million years ago.

When did the first wolverines develop? Scientists don't know. Maybe one day they will find fossils to tell them.

Scientists have found fossils of this early *Plesiogulo* in Ukraine, India, and China.

Wild Word

FOSSIL: Any evidence of ancient life, such as teeth, bones, plant imprints, footprints, eggs, and dung

Scientists have discovered the fossils of an early wolverine. It's called *Plesiogulo* (PLEEZ-ee-oo-GOO-loh). It first appeared on Earth at least 10 million years ago.

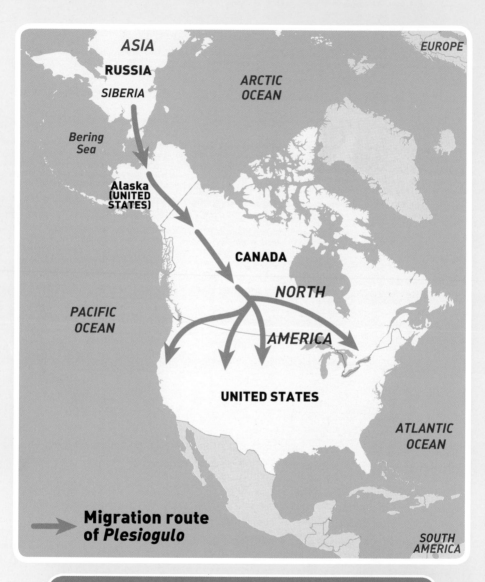

ASIA

RUSSIA

SIBERIA

ARCTIC
OCEAN

EUROPE

Bering
Sea

Alaska
(UNITED
STATES)

CANADA

NORTH

PACIFIC
OCEAN

AMERICA

UNITED STATES

ATLANTIC
OCEAN

**Migration route
of *Plesiogulo***

SOUTH
AMERICA

Today, the Bering Sea separates Asia and North
America, but about seven million years ago a land bridge
linked the two continents. Many animals, including
Plesiogulo, moved back and forth over the land.

This *Plesiogulo* once lived in the United States. It may be the ancestor of today's wolverines.

About seven million years ago, a group of *Plesiogulo* traveled from Asia to North America.

At that time, the sea level was lower than it is today. The world had more land and less ocean area. *Plesiogulo* crossed a strip of land that connected what we now call Russia and Alaska.

Over thousands of years, some wolverines headed east toward the Atlantic Ocean. Others moved south.

At Home With Wolverines

Today, wolverines can be found in chilly northern areas all over the world. And they almost never sit still.

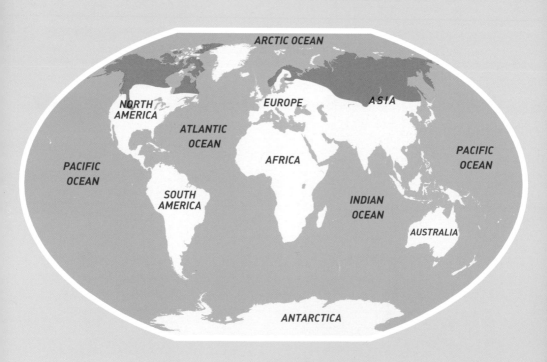

ARCTIC OCEAN

NORTH AMERICA

EUROPE

ASIA

ATLANTIC OCEAN

PACIFIC OCEAN

AFRICA

PACIFIC OCEAN

SOUTH AMERICA

INDIAN OCEAN

AUSTRALIA

ANTARCTICA

■ Where wolverines live

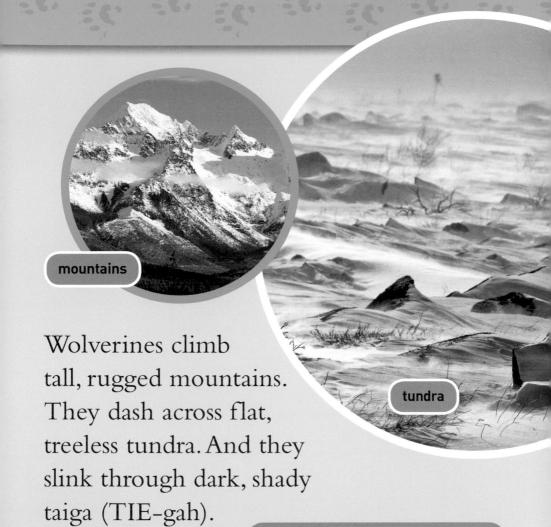

mountains

tundra

Wolverines climb tall, rugged mountains. They dash across flat, treeless tundra. And they slink through dark, shady taiga (TIE-gah).

taiga

Wild Words

TUNDRA: A flat, treeless area in the northern part of the world

TAIGA: A northern forest with trees like pines and spruces

NIFTY NOSE: A wolverine has a keen sense of smell. It can smell a dead body, or carcass, buried under 20 feet of snow. That makes a good meal!

COOL CLAWS: A wolverine's toes have long, sharp claws that grip ice, so the animal doesn't slip and slide. The claws also help a wolverine climb steep mountains.

How can wolverines live in such cold places?

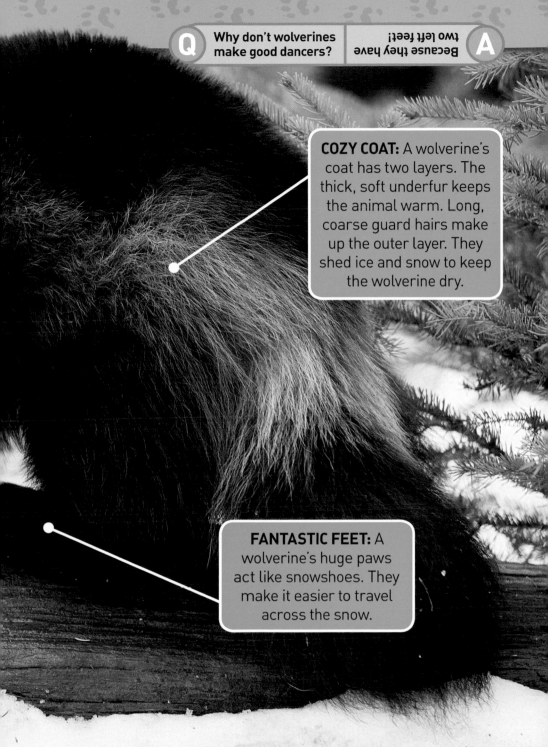

COZY COAT: A wolverine's coat has two layers. The thick, soft underfur keeps the animal warm. Long, coarse guard hairs make up the outer layer. They shed ice and snow to keep the wolverine dry.

FANTASTIC FEET: A wolverine's huge paws act like snowshoes. They make it easier to travel across the snow.

Their bodies are built to survive.

Room to Roam

weird but true!

Male and female wolverines mark the edges of their territories with a stinky fluid. It sends a strong message to other wolverines: "Stay away!"

An adult wolverine spends a lot of time hunting alone. But males and females with overlapping territories do sometimes meet and spend time together. These wolverines often form close bonds and mate with one another.

A wolverine's biggest challenge is finding enough food. What's the solution?

Space. Lots and lots of space. The more room a wolverine has to search for prey, the more likely it is to survive.

A male wolverine's territory is huge. It can be half the size of Rhode Island, U.S.A. It usually overlaps with the territories of two or three females.

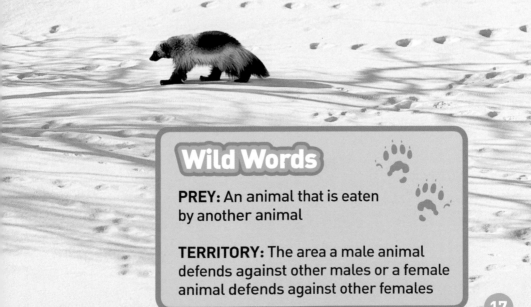

Wild Words

PREY: An animal that is eaten by another animal

TERRITORY: The area a male animal defends against other males or a female animal defends against other females

Imagine walking 500 miles—the distance a car could drive in about nine hours on a highway. Could you do it?

Wolverines can! Scientists tracked one who traveled that far.

Wild Word

TRACK:
To follow

These scientists are tracking a wolverine. Where do you think its footprints will lead?

Many animals can move quickly, but only for a short time. Wolverines are different. They can keep pushing ahead with a steady lope for hours.

Wild Word

LOPE: To move forward with long leaping strides

A wolverine can travel 20 miles in just one day.

What's for Dinner?

A wolverine will eat almost anything it can find. In the summer, it hunts beavers, porcupines, squirrels, rabbits, mice, birds, and fish. It also eats birds' eggs and berries.

weird but true!

The wolverine's scientific name is *Gulo gulo*. *Gulo* is a Latin word that means "glutton," or "greedy eater." That's exactly what a wolverine is.

berries

A wolverine stashes leftovers in cool, hidden spots. Sometimes it digs a hole and buries extra food there.

squirrel

beaver

21

In the winter, wolverines attack moose, caribou, reindeer, and wild sheep that are stuck in deep snow. They search for animals killed by the cold weather.

Wolverines can smell animals hibernating under the snow. They dig down and catch the prey.

Wild Word

HIBERNATING: Spending the winter in a resting state

Terrific Teeth!

A wolverine's teeth can slice through flesh. They can rip apart frozen dead animals. They can even crush bone.

cougar

gray wolf

grizzly bear

Cougars.
Wolves.
Grizzly bears.
A wolverine is smaller than all of these predators. But it's tough, and it's stubborn. It will often try to defend its prey against any of these hungry hunters.

Wild Word

PREDATOR: An animal that hunts and eats other animals

A wolverine is super strong, too. At Denali National Park in Alaska, U.S.A., people spotted a 40-pound wolverine dragging a 150-pound Dall sheep. It tugged the sheep down a rocky mountain slope, across a shallow river, and up a steep bank. It was a two-mile trip. Wow!

Dall sheep

6 COOL THINGS
About Wolverines

Cats and dogs walk on their toes. Their heels stay in the air. But a wolverine's whole foot touches the ground as it moves.

1

2

Wolverines use snow like a refrigerator. They bury meat in the snow to keep it cool and fresh.

A wolverine will do almost anything for food. Scientists watched in amazement as a wolverine scaled a mile-high mountain in just 90 minutes. What was it after? A mountain goat carcass.

3

A hungry wolverine will eat every bit of an animal's body—even its teeth and jaw.

Wolverines are always on the go. They can travel up to 10 miles without taking a rest.

Wolverines can easily climb trees, and they are excellent swimmers.

A Wolverine's Life

A female wolverine's den may be up to 15 feet underground.

Most female wolverines raise a family every other year. In February, they get ready by digging a den in the snow.

The den has at least three rooms and lots of tunnels. There are several doors so the family can make a quick escape if it needs to.

A female wolverine lines her den's sleeping room with shredded wood. She stashes food in the feeding room. Can you guess what the toilet room is for?

A door to the den is just big enough for Mom.

In late winter or early spring, a female gives birth. She has one to four kits.

The kits have soft white fur. Soon, their fur begins to darken. The kits stay in the den for eight to ten weeks.

As the snow melts, the kits head out into the world.

Wild Word

KIT: A young wolverine

These wolverine kits were born at a research facility in Idaho, U.S.A.

Weird but true!

Baby wolverines look like tiny polar bears.

A young kit rambles about when its mama is nearby. But when she goes in search of food, the little one hides in a safe place.

Young wolverines are full of energy. They wrestle, tumble, and nip at each other. Sometimes their dad comes for a visit and joins in the fun.

After playtime, the kits start exploring. *Sniff, sniff. Chomp!* They smell and taste everything in sight.

For these kits, the Rocky Mountains of Montana, U.S.A., are a great place to grow up.

Two wolverines travel together through an open forest in northern Europe.

A young wolverine stops depending on its mom when it's about six months old. But it stays within its parents' territories for another year.

During this time, it may explore with its brother or sister. Once in a while, it visits its parents. It may hunt with its mom or travel with its dad for a few days.

When a wolverine is about two years old, it leaves its parents' territory. It may have to travel a long distance to find a new home. Then it can start a family of its own.

In Finland, a young wolverine may travel for miles across the taiga in search of its own territory.

Studying Wolverines

Scientists are beginning to understand the wolverine way of life. They are slowly making progress.

But they don't know as much about wolverines as they would like to. It's hard to study these animals.

PROBLEM: Wolverines live in cold places that are hard to reach.

SOLUTION: Scientists use cross-country skis. Sometimes they travel through fierce snowstorms.

PROBLEM: Wolverines are smart. They can escape from most traps.

SOLUTION: Scientists build special log traps. They also collect wolverine fur with hair snares. They can learn a lot by testing the hairs.

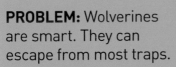

A scientist removes fur from a hair snare.

Two scientists add fresh bait to a camera trap.

PROBLEM: Wolverines are feisty. They tear off radio collars used to track most animals.

SOLUTION: Scientists track wolverines by placing sensors inside the animals' bodies. They also use camera traps to catch wolverines in action.

Facing the Future

Wolverines are smart and strong. They're feisty and fierce. They're curious and caring. And most of all, they never give up.

These traits have helped wolverines survive for millions of years. But now they're in trouble.

Scientists worry that 50 percent of Earth's tundra and taiga will disappear in the next 50 years. If that happens, at least half of the world's wolverines may disappear, too.

Gases rise into the air when fossil fuels burn. These gases are causing our planet to heat up.

As people burn fossil fuels to make electricity and power their cars, the world is heating up. That's bad news for animals that need to live in cold places.

Wild Word

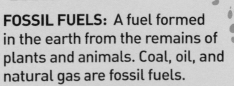

FOSSIL FUELS: A fuel formed in the earth from the remains of plants and animals. Coal, oil, and natural gas are fossil fuels.

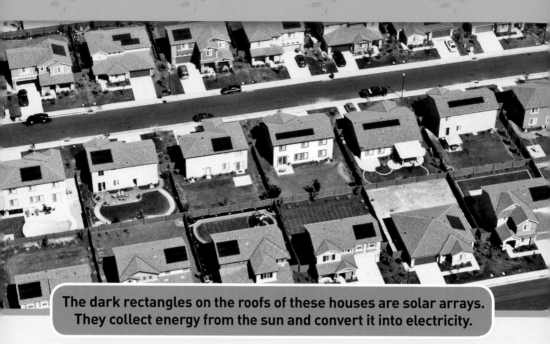

The dark rectangles on the roofs of these houses are solar arrays. They collect energy from the sun and convert it into electricity.

Luckily, there is still hope. We can work together to slow down global warming.

Some people are now using solar power in their homes. Others are using wind power. These changes are a big help. But simple things can make a difference, too.

If we make changes now, we can help wolverines live far into the future.

Five Simple Ways You Can Help

You can reduce the amount of fossil fuels you use by:

1. Turning off the lights when you leave a room.

2. Turning off TVs and computers when you aren't using them.

3. Using your car less. Walk, ride your bike, take the bus, or carpool with a friend.

4. Putting on a sweater instead of turning up the heat.

5. Turning down the heat or air-conditioning when no one is home.

QUIZ WHIZ

How much do you know about wolverines? After reading this book, probably a lot! Take this quiz and find out.

Answers are at the bottom of page 45.

Wolverines are closely related to _____.

A. wolves
B. weasels
C. armadillos
D. bears

Which of the following statements is not true?

A. A wolverine's feet help it survive.
B. A wolverine's paws act like snowshoes.
C. A wolverine's long, sharp claws grip the ice.
D. A wolverine walks on its toes like a cat.

A wolverine can _____ nonstop for hours.

A. scamper
B. gallop
C. hop
D. lope

4

Gulo is a Latin word. What does it mean?

A. greedy
B. feisty
C. clever
D. strong

A wolverine will often try to defend its food against a _____.

A. bear
B. cougar
C. wolf
D. all of the above

5

6

What do young wolverines do when they no longer depend on their mom?

A. spend all their time with their dad
B. immediately find their own territory
C. stay in their parents' territories for about a year
D. none of the above

Why are wolverines difficult to study?

A. Scientists don't know where they live.
B. They can escape from most traps.
C. Scientists don't know how to track them.
D. All of the above.

7

Answers: 1. B; 2. D; 3. D; 4. A; 5. D; 6. C; 7. B

45

Glossary

FOSSIL: Any evidence of ancient life, such as teeth, bones, plant imprints, footprints, eggs, and dung

KIT: A young wolverine

LOPE: To move forward with long leaping strides

TAIGA: A northern forest with trees like pines and spruces

TERRITORY: The area a male animal defends against other males or a female animal defends against other females

FOSSIL FUELS: A fuel formed in the earth from the remains of plants and animals. Coal, oil, and natural gas are fossil fuels.

HIBERNATING: Spending the winter in a resting state

PREDATOR: An animal that hunts and eats other animals

PREY: An animal that is eaten by another animal

TRACK: To follow

TUNDRA: A flat, treeless area in the northern part of the world